Pushkin

Minds the Bundle

by
HARRIET M. ZIEFERT

paintings by
DONALD SAAF

AN ANNE SCHWARTZ BOOK

ATHENEUM BOOKS *for* YOUNG READERS

For Nathaniel Isaac Ziefert
—H. M. Z.

For Ole and Isak and for all our friends
in Guysborough County, Nova Scotia
—D. S.

Atheneum Books for Young Readers
An imprint of Simon & Schuster Children's Publishing Division
1230 Avenue of the Americas
New York, New York 10020

Book design by Michael Nelson

The text of this book is set in Stempel Schneidler.
The illustrations are rendered in gouache.

Printed in China for Harriet Ziefert, Inc.
2 4 6 8 10 9 7 5 3 1

Library of Congress Cataloging-in-Publication Data:
Ziefert, Harriet.
Pushkin minds the bundle / by Harriet M. Ziefert; illustrated by Donald Saaf.   p. cm.
"An Anne Schwartz Book."
Summary: Pushkin the dog is initially jealous of the new baby in the household, but eventually they reconcile their differences.
ISBN 0-689-83216-8
[1. Dogs—Fiction. 2. Babies—Fiction.] I. Saaf, Donald, ill. II. Title.
PZ7.Z487Pud   2000   [E]—dc21   99-27578

FIRST
EDITION

Remember me? I'm Pushkin.

Here I am with Kate and Michael and the baby.
They call him Pierre, but I think of him as "the bundle."

We're going on vacation.

Pierre gets fussy on long rides, so he gets everything
he wants. The best seat. The windows closed.
Music that *he* likes. And all the snacks he can eat!

Kate says to me, "Pushkin, you're my big boy.
It's your job to mind Pierre."
Can't she see that I *do* mind him? I mind him a lot!

Still, I sing.

I make funny faces.

I pick up his toys.

But sometimes I don't
feel like being so nice.

At last, Michael pulls into a rest stop.
Thank goodness, we can go to the bathroom.

And we can run!

We drive, and drive, and drive some more.
Are we there yet? I want to know.
"Quiet down, boy," says Michael. "Quiet!"

Finally, we're there! Kate says, "Pushkin, you mind
Pierre while we unpack."
I don't want to mind him. Why can't *he* mind himself?

"This bedroom is for you and Pierre," says Kate.
I want the red bed, but the bundle wants it too.

When he starts to cry, Kate says, "Now, Pushkin.
Be good. You take the blue bed."
I make a BIG, BIG FUSS . . .

. . . and I get the blue bed!
Our first night is no fun. Maybe it's
because of the mice, who scratch.

Or maybe it's the cold, creaky beds.
After awhile, I crawl into the red bed with the
bundle. We keep each other warm.

In the morning, we go fishing. Lucky for me, the bundle is too little to come. I hold on to my line for a long time, but nothing happens.

So I jump overboard.

And look!

On a different vacation day, Michael
and Kate take us blueberry-picking.

Here we are, trudging along.

Michael and Kate fill their pails with berries.
Me and the bundle—we EAT lots of berries!

Sometimes, Pierre gets just the one I want.
And we fight.

While we're busy, the bundle wanders off.

"Pushkin, where's Pierre?" Kate asks.
I feel like saying, "I don't know where he is.
I don't *care* where he is."

But I want to find him.

AND I DO!

Michael pats my nose. "Pushkin, you have a good sniffer. Nice work, big boy."

Kate gives me a big kiss. I'm glad I found the bundle.

Here we are on our last night, roasting marshmallows and singing. Pierre's too small to sing, so I'm the star of the show.

Michael and Kate like my melancholy tunes.
I'm sure Pierre does, too.

It's sad when a vacation ends.
But Michael and Kate say we can come again.
And maybe I won't have to mind the bundle.

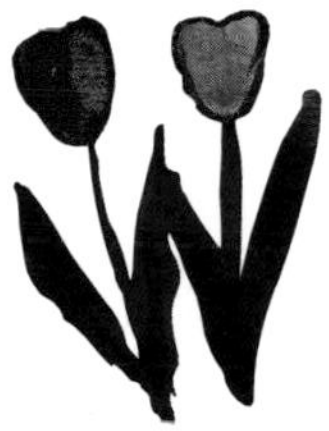